THE BOOK

MAKE YOUR
DREAMS
COME TRUE

Diamond Mountain University Press

dmu-press.com

Diamond Mountain University Press
dmu-press.com

The Book

Published in the United States by Diamond Mountain University Press
Visit our website at www.dmu-press.com

ISBN-978-0-9837478-5-7

PRINTED IN THE UNITED STATES OF AMERICA

2 0 1 1 0 7 0 0 0 1

More by Geshe Michael Roach:

The Principal Teachings of Buddhism (author Je Tsongkapa, compiler Geshe Michael Roach)

Preparing for Tantra: The Mountain of Blessings (authors Je Tsongkapa, Geshe Michael Roach, Lobsang Tharchin)

The Diamond Cutter:
The Buddha on Managing Your Business and Your Life

The Garden: A Parable

How Yoga Works: Healing Yourself and Others with the Yoga Sutra

The Essential Yoga Sutra: Ancient Wisdom for Your Yoga

The Tibetan Book of Yoga:
Ancient Buddhist Teachings on the Philosophy and Practice of Yoga

The Eastern Path to Heaven:
A Guide to Happiness from the Teachings of Jesus in Tibet

Karmic Management:
 What Goes Around Comes Around in Your Business and Your Life

Instructions on how to Keep
THE BOOK

Based on a teaching by
Geshe Michael Roach

How To Keep The Book

Very quickly, I want to teach you how to do The Book. Some people want to call it a "confession book." I don't like that. That's the old days, okay? Some people want to call it a "purification book." That's okay. Some people want to call it a "getting-to-paradise-book." I like that a lot. I always did like positive reinforcement better. Some people want to call it a "six-times-a-day book," which I think may be best because then you don't forget the main quality of this book which is that you do it six times a day.

In the morning after I brush my teeth, blow my nose, and get some tea or juice, one of the first things I do is load my book for the day. It's a very nice habit.

Get a blank book, something you will enjoy writing in. Take the book, open it up, on the left page draw a vertical line down the middle and two horizontal lines across making six equal boxes.* Six times a day you're going to stop, open up this little book and write down how you're doing.

Six times a day you stop and you do your Book. This is the way to get to heaven. This is the way that Buddhism works. If you keep going to classes for years nothing big will happen to you. You need to meditate every day and you must check your heart six times a day, or it just doesn't work. Nothing happens. You may have met lots of Americans who are professional Dharma students who, even though we can't judge other people, it would seem that they haven't progressed at all since the beginning, years back. So I think you must examine your heart six times a day. It must be part of your Buddhism. It is probably the most important part of your Buddhism, okay? So six times a day you check your vows. How many vows do you have? Every Buddhist is trying to keep "The Ten." I'll give them to you right now. If you don't have any others just watch these ten. I like to state them in a positive way:

1) Did you protect life today? In some form. Did you move a pencil

* see pg 16

off the stairway that someone might have slipped on? You're not going to get a chance to throw someone out of the way of a speeding taxi or invent the Salk vaccine every day. Did you give aspirin to someone at work? Did you make tea for someone with a sniffle? This is protecting life. The karmic result of checking this one every day is that your body will get light, strong, healthy—unbelievable. Just little things! The Book is made for little things. The Book is made for moving a pencil off the stairway where you live. So that's protecting life.

2) Honor other people's property. Did you make noise today going up the stairs? Did you take the last of the toilet paper from the bathroom and not make sure that the next person had some? Stuff like that—small. Heaven is built on small things. You'll find out that you don't have to be Mother Teresa. It's the state of your mind. Your state of mind has to be concerned about details. It's the small things that make you a perfect spiritual person. Seriously.

3) Sexual Purity. Are you faithful in your relationships with other people? If you are engaging in sex, are you doing it at a nice, normal, healthy level and not getting obsessed about it or thinking about it all day, or doing it in improper places at improper times, and with improper people? A healthy sexual, normal, relationship—fine. Adultery, all sorts of weird things, not fine, okay? Does it bother your peace of mind? See what I mean? That's the question. And maintain the level of sexual purity that you've committed to.

For a married person it would be, did you check out someone's wife today? Just for a second, did you do that?
Something like that, all right? This person is already committed to another. Are you honoring that relationship by not bothering that person's spouse, even in your mind? Sex is similar to eating. There is overeating, there is eating bad food, there is eating what you need, there is eating what's good for you; and finally in Buddhism there is a stage where you don't need to eat any more, and sex is exactly the same. It's just a progression of a spectrum. The goal is to get to a point where you don't

need it for the human body. It is a psychological thing that you can supply through much more amazing means, okay? Generally work towards that. That's all. Don't get guilty, don't feel bad, don't feel dirty. Right now it's a normal healthy thing. Do it nicely, don't let it obsess your life. Do it nicely, beautifully, and in a sensitive way. Don't get close to adultery and hurting other people's relationships. That's the main thing right now. Honor your own and other people's commitments and don't ever cross that line.

4) Try to be totally truthful all day long. So, are you required to tell someone how bad their dress looks who asks you for your opinion? Change the subject, okay? Drop your coffee cup. If it would hurt the person in some terrible way, make them very angry, if it's very destructive, you can just sort of slide out of it.

5) Do you speak in ways that you try to bring people together? Do you, in your everyday conversations, try to bring people close together? Once in a while you meet a person who's really good at this. I have a friend, he'll run up to you and say, "I got a person for you! I've got someone who you've got to meet! You'll love this person!" He introduces you and you're best friends forever. Do you see what I mean? Because our normal human tendency is, "Did you hear what he said about you? Oh! You don't wanna know." So it's doing the opposite. It is concentrating on doing the opposite, okay? Bringing people together with your words.

6) Speak gently to other people. Use gentle speech when you speak to other people. Gentle, thoughtful; no curse words unless they're your best friends. We had names for our roommates in college (that I can't tell you) and they were meant in a nice, beautiful way. Then there are ways of talking to people in sweet ways when you're not feeling sweet at all. Like when you say "have a nice day," but what you really mean is "go to hell." It is judged by your intent. Speak gently for the context.

7) Try to speak meaningfully. Whenever you open your mouth, try to say something that has some kind of relevance to the person's life. Like, don't sit there and blab about the latest gossip or stuff that's never going to be resolved. Stuff that doesn't matter, stuff that doesn't help anybody. Don't talk about politics or other people's problems or just waste talk, okay? When you open your mouth say something meaningful.

8) When you see someone else get something nice, be happy. What's the opposite of that? It's like jealousy or unhappiness when somebody gets something nice. When something good happens to somebody else, you rush up and say, "I'm so happy you got that promotion! I can't believe it! You really deserve it." Something like that—consciously trying to take joy in other people's successes. Our human tendency is to be jealous. We say, "We are bodhisattvas, we are Mahayana Buddhists. We are committed to the goal of bringing every happiness to every sentient being." So don't think, "I don't see why the hell they got the promotion."

9) Try to feel for other people who have a misfortune. Like when someone has a misfortune, you take the time and the effort to try and empathize with them. You try to go to them and say "I'm sorry that happened to you." The normal human tendency is to do the opposite. "Have you heard about [some famous person], he murdered somebody, his life is ruined? Tell me more!" There's this human tendency to be fascinated by other people's problems, especially famous people's problems. "150 passengers died? Ooo, how? Did the fuselage break up or not?" You know what I mean? This is the big thing in the newspapers, and people are dying to know about it. You have to think the opposite. When you hear about something like that, you're like, "Oh, I'm sorry for his family, and I feel really bad about it and I wish that wouldn't happen to anyone." It's the opposite of being fascinated by other people's problems. You truly try to put yourself in their place and try to help them out with their problems. It's extensive empathy or compassion for other people's problems rather than this secret little joy. Okay?

If you work in a corporation, and I worked in a corporation for 16 years, the opposite goes on very frequently. Somebody makes a $100,000 error on a shipment, and you're not going to get a raise this year because of it, and you're still fascinated. You're like "tell me, how did he do it?" It's a weird human tendency. You know? You're not upset by it, you are fascinated by it. "Tell me, how did he screw up, how did it get stolen? They went to the wrong address?" You know it's gonna ruin your raise too, but you don't care. You're just fascinated.

10) Maintain a Buddhist World View. Understand all good things come from helping other people, and all bad things come from watching out for your own interest only. You can watch out for your own interests, but equally watch out for other people's interests. That's healthy. Okay? At the expense of others, you serve yourself. That's a wrong Buddhist view. Every good thing in the world—money, financial security, friends, relationships, food, chocolate milk shakes, everything comes from serving other people. That's the Buddhist belief. You cannot breathe one breath of air unless you helped someone in the past to live. The reason you have the honor of breathing for the rest of today is that each breath comes from having done something for someone else, like making food. That's the Buddhist World View. You strive to keep it.

These are the top ten out of 84,000. These ten are going through your mind every few hours. What they're saying is that the opposite goes through your mind every few hours. They ruin your life, they make you unhappy. You wish for yourself to be happy, and for others to have happiness also. Wanting it for yourself is fine as long as you go about getting it in a nice healthy Dharma way. Okay? Which normally means giving it away to someone else. Sorry. By the way, then you get it back ten-fold. Guaranteed. So it's no big sweat.

Now you've got ten vows, right? Those of you who have Refuge, you've got 22 vows because you have 12 Refuge commitments. Those of you who have Bodhisattva vows have 86 plus a bunch of other ones. Those of you who have tantric vows have 484 commitments. Okay? You don't check 484 vows a day, you check six. And you cycle through them.

If you have ten vows, at eight in the morning you start with number 1: "Did I honor life?" Okay? You put vow number one, honoring life, protecting life, in the first box.* Then at eight in the morning you put a **plus (+), a minus (-)**, and a **to do** in the first box. The second box is for 10:30. The third box is for 12:00. The fourth is for 3:00, because you got busy. The fifth box is for 5-ish, and the last box is for 7:00.

Every two to three hours you're checking the next vow, the next commitment. So what do you write down for honoring life? You put down a **positive (+)**. Why do we do the positive first? In case you die between lines, you at least die with some good karma on your mind. Okay? This will protect you if you die before you get to the negative, which one day you will. Your positive has to be a specific occurrence, today or yesterday that really happened; that had to do with your success in honoring life. Um... got Fabrizio a carrot juice. Okay? This is a real example from an hour ago, I could have ordered him a coke, but I'm seeing that this guy looks healthy, let's keep him healthy, order him a carrot juice. No more glorious than that. No Mother Teresa stuff, no Mahatma Gandhi stuff. This is what you get enlightened on. I'm not kidding, real life. Real life minor examples that are really happening to you. You keep up your Buddhist principles at this microcosmic level, and you'll be a saint in quick order. It's the small things that make saints. You only get a chance to be Joan of Arc once in a lifetime. The rest of the time she milked the cows, right? Enlightenment is built on these minor specific things that you do.

You only do six vows a day. You're gonna do one to six the first day, do seven through two (7, 8, 9, 10, 1, 2) the next day, then three through eight (3, 4, 5, 6, 7, 8) the following day. Like that. You're cycling through. You do six today of your ten. Tomorrow you start with seven, and when you get to ten you start over again with one. If you are tracking the bodhisattva vows you do six, one through six, then seven through 12, then 13 through..., 'till you get to the end of the 64 vows. Then you go back again.

Bottom line, you take all the vows you currently have, add them all up, and just go through them until you get to the end. Six a day. Is that easy? Okay? So you're only checking one different vow every two-and-a-half hours. And you're rotating through the total number of vows that you have. For me, 484 vows, one rotation takes about 80 days. Takes me about two-and-a-half months to get back to the first vow. That's fine. Okay? That's the way it's supposed to work.

Q: If you're at work and all of a sudden two hours go by and you haven't thought about any vows, haven't broken any of them, what should you do?

Geshe Michael: If you're at work and real busy, you can use something of the principle of free association. You must use it. Like did I commit adultery in the last two hours? Come on, I was too busy, I had a business meeting and there were no girls there. You know what I mean? Well then, on the way to work did you look at somebody that you didn't know? Was she married or not? Free associate. Did you open the National Inquirer and waste some time looking at the girl in an ad? Something like that. In monastic vows it's called the concentric circle theory. (see next page)

In the center is committing adultery. The next level is, oh let's say touching them. Then sitting with them alone, you know in a room. Next is looking at them or staying close to them. Then talking to them more than is appropriate. Next is looking at someone else's wife. On the outside is looking at sexy ads in the magazine. For a monk, we try never to break the outside one and then you've got no problem not breaking the inside one. This is the circle theory of breaking your vows. If you never look at an advertisement of a printed lady, you'll never go further than that. See what I mean? And so free associate backwards 'til you hit something.

Did I protect life? No. Did I offer any carrot juice in the last 24 hours? No. How about 48 hours? There was that one thing that I did.

The negative (-) would be something like, didn't get enough sleep last night. Anything you did to hurt yourself counts. You are one of the sentient beings in the universe. You're supposed to take care of yourself too. So, didn't get enough sleep; ate more ice-cream than I comfortably could. Something that hurt you or someone else.

"To do" is a very, very specific small thing that you can do in next 24 to 48 hours. Go to bed on time tonight. Something like that. Clean the shelves in the bathroom because roaches can get in there and get killed when I leave my coffee cup in there. Get down to that kind of morality.

According to the concentric circle theory you'll be keeping every-

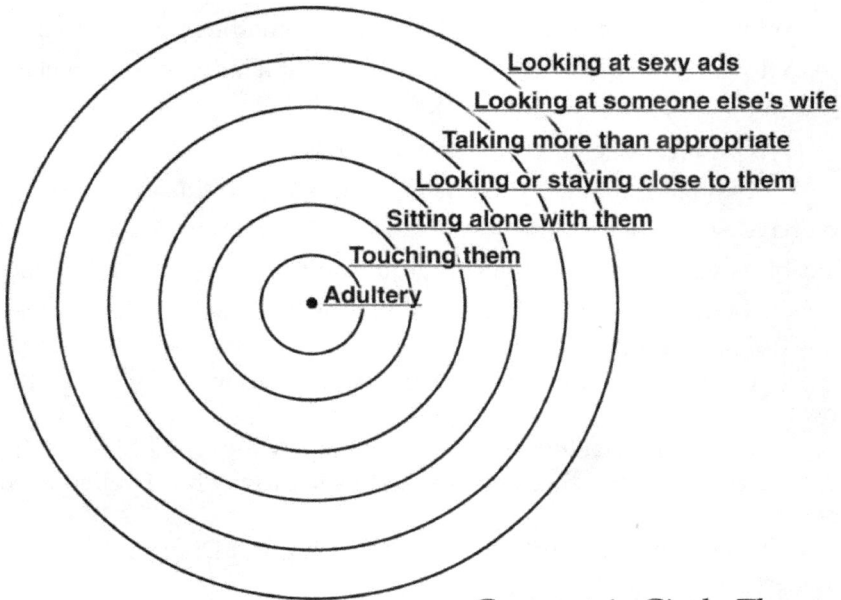

Looking at sexy ads
Looking at someone else's wife
Talking more than appropriate
Looking or staying close to them
Sitting alone with them
Touching them
Adultery

Concentric Circle Theory

thing very purely if you do this. People don't understand the way to be a perfect being. The way to reach tantric enlightenment is to keep this dumb little thing. This is a tantric vow. I am breaking a tantric vow. I'm telling you one of my tantric vows. In the highest levels of tantra you do this thing six times a day called *tundruk*, you must check six times a day. Why is it a tantric vow? Because if you do this thing you'll get your rear end into a tantric paradise before you die. Why? Because your morality is down to nuts and bolts, real life, specific things that are happening.

Don't put in the **negative (-)** "I am a bad person." Don't put "I like chocolate." It's gotta be something specific; "I ate one chocolate this afternoon." And the to do is: "No matter what happens in the next three hours, I'm not going to eat any chocolate," even if you're gonna eat one four hours from now.

Morality starts small, self-control starts small. Okay? Three hours of self-control is a good start. It's enough. It's more than you ever did before. And you'll find if you keep this up after a couple of months your self-control becomes incredible. Don't put something unreasonable in the to do. Don't say, "I will never again look at a lady on the street." Do something really reasonable.

Q: Can I check the Bodhisattva vows?

Geshe Michael: If you wish to follow the Bodhisattva vows, and you have any source for the vows, and want to start checking them now, God bless you! That's wonderful! You don't have to have bodhisattva vows to be checking them from time to time. Follow them to the best of your understanding.

Q: What if I can't find anything specific to write for one of the vows?

Geshe Michael: If you have trouble finding something specific, free associate. I didn't threaten any body's life today but I yelled at so and so.

Q: What about the vow, "giving up the highest Dharma of the listener's way?"

Geshe Michael: I have trouble with that one too. Free associate like crazy and then learn more about the vow. In that vow there's a list of 20 different ideas the Listeners have, but which you just haven't studied deeply enough yet. It happens to be that the teaching on the Four Arya Truths is what they are talking about. If you still think that getting a promotion at work would be the end of the truth of suffering, which is one of the Four Arya Truths, than you're not respecting the Listener's path. Something like that. You just need to learn more about the vow.

Q: What if there is nothing recent? Should I go back years?

Geshe Michael: No, try to find something specific, recent, okay. Last 24 hours, 48 hours, or a week, something like that. If you have some really old bad ones like an abortion or something, throw that in every once in a while.

You check your book six times a day, every two-and-a-half hours. It's no good to get to the end of the day and do five of them. That belabors the point. Okay? It's wrong. There's a corruption of the tantric verse where they do it twice a day and they repeat it three times. That's bad. The guy who invented it said, "I'm doing this for retarded people only." It says that at the end of the text but people skip that part. Seriously, I'm not kidding. Okay, you've got the idea. Six times.

Q: What if I forget to do a vow or my book that day?

Geshe Michael: If you slip, you have to finish it. But don't slip. I worked in a corporation. I had three telephones, I had 400 people working for me. I just went to the bathroom. I found out that no one ever challenged me if I went to the bathroom. I could have 12 people standing in a line outside my door and I said "I gotta poop guys." No one ever asked me "Stay, stay!" (until I got to my Dharma students,) but ah, anyway, just go. I have lots of friends who are executives and they keep their book in their calendar so they don't look Buddhist at work, and I did the same thing, take it out, go to the stall, close the door, you know, write it out. Really. I've been in huge board meetings, and millions of dollars flying around, and just got up and said I gotta go.

Q: When do you write down the vows?

Geshe Michael: I do them in the morning when I have time. I drink a cup of tea before my meditation and I try to enjoy it, and get it all loaded in the morning. I write out all the vows for the day.

On the right side of the book, about half way down make a **T**, to make two columns. In the left column you put **one, two, three,** and in the right column **one, two, three.*** What is this for? Let's say that tomorrow you will be doing vows seven through two, if you only have ten vows. You have already done one through six today. So you won't be doing vow number one tomorrow, which is what? Protecting life. Now suppose you happened to have killed your boss that day and it doesn't come up in the six boxes. That means for 24 hours that you're going to have that karma on your hands. Karma exponentially increases every 24 hours. The karma of killing your boss on Wednesday if you don't write it down is the karma of killing two bosses by Thursday, and four bosses by Friday and 16 bosses by Saturday. I'm not kidding. This is the

* see pg 17

principle of how karma increases. You've got to write it down the same day. So this section of **The Book** is reserved for the end of the day. You list the best three, worst three things you did that day. You review your whole day and put down the best three on the left, and the worst three on the right. Go over your day just before you go to sleep. Purify your three negatives and rejoice in your three positives. It's very good to die with a clear conscience. If you die during your sleep it is very good to have done your book before you die. Okay, put the best three on the left, and the worst three on the right. They could be included in the vows you reviewed during the day. If you did a really crappy thing that's included there, then add it at the end of the day too. If you did a really crappy thing that didn't come in your vows that day make sure to put it down as one of these three.

Q: Even if I didn't have that vow that day?
Geshe Michael: Right. Just in case you killed
your boss and there's no killing vow that day.
So you don't get out of it.

Draw a horizontal line dividing the remaining space at the top of the right page.* I save this middle box for special things, and meditation. How did my meditation go today? That forces you to report on something that you gotta do. If it's blank it means you didn't do it or else it was a totally unexciting meditation. I make notes, like "Figured out that I should push the pillow up a half inch; did tonglen on that schmuck at work." I force myself to make a note about it. You can put special stuff in there that you're having problems with, like if you tend to get angry at a certain person, have an entry in there for a week or two. You know, "How am I doing with this person?"

In the last box at the very top draw a vertical line in the middle of it.* The box on the left is reserved for ordained vows I have a whole separate system going on for my monks vows. Because most of the American sangha don't know their vows very well, it's very useful to write your

* see pg 17

vows down specifically and cycle through your monks and nuns vows every day. And then you get really good at knowing your vows and you keep them much better. If you don't have monastic vows you can put the five lifetime lay vows here. Do one a day and rotate through the five in that way.

Any questions about the book?

Q: What do you do when you have finished a **Book**?

Geshe Michael: When you fill it in, it is a custom in Tibet to throw it into a forest, or into a river. Bodies of water are supposed to be holy. You can take them to the sea. Save them up for a couple of months, go to the beach throw them in. Don't get caught. Go to the Hudson river, throw it in. It's considered auspicious to offer like that. You might want to save them for a year or two and go back and see how you're doing. Sometimes you can get a lot of information 6 months later. You go back and you ask what was my screwy mind thinking, what was I having problems with six months ago? And then you notice that you're still having the same problem. Personally I save them, I've got probably 50 of them or so. And it's wonderful. It's really wonderful. You really, really change. Just by observing your self, you change. It's wonderful and your mind starts to change totally, and then your world starts to change.

Last question.

Q: Do you write down the date?

Geshe Michael: I like to date them. I date it, and mark down the full moon. At full moon something actually does happen. I put down stuff like that. Also a lot of my students mark the time down for each vow just so they make sure they remember it. I've got students who are about to reach nirvana. I've got one I can specifically think of. She recently wrote me, "as of next week I'll have kept my book for two years. I have never missed an entry and I have never been late with an entry." And this person is like so high she can barely touch the ground. It works, it really works!

* *see pg 17*

Q: Where do you get these different lists of vows and the explanations of them?

Geshe Michael: The morality vows are explained in the Vinaya course, the Asian Classics Institute Correspondence Course number nine. The bodhisattva vows are explained exhaustively like no one has ever explained them in Correspondence Course number seven. For tantric vows you have to ask your tantric teacher to give them to you.

Remember, pick a time of the day that you're going to do your meditation and stick with it every single day, no matter what. Do your book and you will be happy forever. You will see a tantric paradise in this lifetime. But you've gotta do it. The longer you wait the more delay you'll have. It's not like this stupid obligation thing, or something Geshe Michael's forcing you to do. This is your ticket to paradise. Truly, really! Your reality will start to change because your reality is determined by what you do and say during the day. Your reality in six months is totally created by what you do now. You can change your reality in six months from now. You can change the crime rate in New York. You can change your credit card. Everything! It all depends upon how you act today. That's what Buddhism says, so do it! Don't think of it as an obligation or some stupid thing. Don't fight it, just do it.

**EVERYTHING YOU EVER
DREAMED OF WILL COME TRUE.**

The Book

1. Protecting life   *8:00 am*
      (refrain from killing)

+

−

to do

2. Honoring other's property   *10:30 am*
      (refrain from stealing)

+

−

to do

3. Sexual Purity   *12:00 pm*
      (refrain from sexual misconduct)

+

−

to do

4. Being totally truthful   *3:00 pm*
      (refrain from lying)

+

−

to do

5. Speaking in ways to bring   *5:00 pm*
   others together
    (refrain from divisive speech)

+

−

to do

6. Speaking gently   *7:00 pm*
      (refrain from harsh words)

+

−

to do

The Book

Monastic Vows,
or Lifetime Lay Vows

Date:

Special reminders

Meditation:

Best	Worst
1.	1.
2.	2.
3.	3.

THE VOWS

The Book

I. THE REFUGE COMMITMENTS

[1] Not seeking refuge in worldly objects and deities once you have taken refuge in the Buddha

[2] Not harming any living being once you have taken refuge in the Dharma

[3] Not associating closely with people who do not believe in the Path once you have taken refuge in the Sangha

[4] Considering any representation of the Buddha, regardless of the quality of its artistry or material, as though it were the Buddha himself, once you have taken refuge in the Buddha

[5] Considering any written material at all, from a single letter on up, as though it were the Dharma itself, once you have taken refuge in the Dharma

[6] Considering even a single scrap of the saffron robe as though it were the Sangha itself, once you have taken refuge in the Sangha

[7] Going for refuge over and over again, by calling to mind the good qualities of the refuge objects

[8] In remembrance of their kindness, offering the first part of any food or drink to the refuge objects

[9] Encouraging others to take refuge

[10] Taking refuge three times each day, and three times each night, by bringing to mind the benefits of doing so

[11] Putting all your trust in the objects of refuge, during any activity you may undertake at all

[12] Not giving up the Three Jewels, even if it should cost you your life, and in every situation from that on down to doing so in jest

The Book

II. THE VOWS OF FREEDOM

Refraining from

[13] Killing

[14] Stealing

[15] Sexual misconduct

[16] Lying

[17] Divisive talk

[18] Harsh words

[19] Useless talk

[20] Craving

[21] Ill-will

[20] Wrong views

III. THE VOWS OF THE BODHISATTVA

A. ROOT DOWNFALLS

[23] Praising yourself, out of attachment to gain or honor

[24] Criticizing others, out of attachment to gain or honor

[25] Failing to give Dharma, due to feelings of possessiveness

[26] Failing to give material assistance, due to feelings of possessiveness

[27] Failing to accept someone's apology

[28] Striking another

[29] Giving up the greater way

[30] Teaching false Dharma

[31] Stealing what belongs to the Buddha Jewel

[32] Stealing what belongs to the Dharma Jewel

[33] Stealing what belongs to the Sangha Jewel

[34] Giving up the highest Dharma by discounting the scriptural collections of the way of the listeners

[35] Giving up the highest Dharma by discounting the scriptural collections of the way of the self–made Buddhas

[36] Giving up the highest Dharma by discounting the scriptural collections of the greater way

[37] Taking away the golden robes, beating, or incarcerating an ordained person

[38] Removing someone from the status of an ordained person

[39] Committing the immediate misdeed of killing your father

[40] Committing the immediate misdeed of killing your mother

[41] Committing the immediate misdeed of killing an enemy destroyer

[42] Committing the immediate misdeed of creating a schism in the Sangha

[43] Committing the immediate misdeed of drawing blood from a Buddha with evil intent

[44] Holding wrong views

[45] Destroying towns

[46] Destroying cities

[47] Destroying whole areas

[48] Destroying entire countries

[49] Teaching emptiness to a person who is not yet mentally prepared

[50] Causing a person to turn back from total enlightenment

[51] Causing a person to give up the morality of freedom

[52] Holding that a person cannot eliminate desire and the rest by following the way of the learner

[53] Criticizing someone else due to one's desire for the adulation of others

[54] Professing the complete opposite by saying you have seen emptiness directly when you have not

[55] Accepting what belongs to the Jewels, to the Sangha, or to an individual monk when someone presents it to you

[56] Rejecting the practice of quietude, and giving the possessions of meditators to those whose practice is recitation

[57] Discarding the wish for enlightenment

B. SECONDARY OFFENSES

[58] Failing to make offerings to the Jewels through the three doors of expression

[59] Allowing thoughts of desire to go on

[60] Failing to pay respect to those who have taken the precepts of the bodhisattva before you

[61] Failing to answer questions, out of anger or laziness

[62] Failing to accept an invitation, out of pride, or a wish to hurt someone, anger, or laziness

[63] Failing to accept gold or silver or any other kind of material wealth that a sponsor has tried to offer to you, out of a desire to hurt them, or out of anger or laziness

[64] Failing to give the Dharma to those who wish it, out of a desire to hurt them, or out of anger or envy or laziness

[65] Rejecting persons with sullied morality, out of feelings of wanting to hurt them, or out of anger or laziness

[66] Failing to follow the rules of the teachings on discipline which lead other persons to develop faith

[67] Performing deeds which are only of lesser benefit for all living beings

[68] Failing to break a rule out of compassion [There are extraordinary requirements for those who should undertake these kinds of actions, and these must be studied seriously from a qualified Lama before one attempts them.]

[69] Taking up wrong livelihood of trying to obtain things through pretending

[70] Taking up wrong livelihood of trying to obtain things through flattering

[71] Taking up wrong livelihood of trying to obtain things through hinting

[72] Taking up wrong livelihood of trying to obtain things through forcing

[73] Taking up wrong livelihood of trying to obtain things through baiting

[74] Forgetting yourself and acting wild, or getting others to act wild, and so on

[75] Thinking that you only have to travel through the circle of suffering life

[76] Failing to put a stop to rumors about yourself

[77] Failing to correct someone when it must be done in a negative way

[78] Losing the four points of the practice of virtue by responding to scolding with scolding

[79] Losing the four points of the practice of virtue by responding to anger with anger

[80] Losing the four points of the practice of virtue by responding to being beaten by beating

[81] Losing the four points of the practice of virtue by responding to being criticized by criticizing

[82] Simply ignoring those who are angry at you, by failing to explain yourself to them in an appropriate manner out of a desire to hurt them, or pride, or laziness

[83] Refusing to forgive another person when they apologize for doing something wrong to you, out of a desire to hurt them, thoughts of malice, or simply because you don't feel like it

[84] Allowing thoughts of anger to go on

[85] Collecting a group of disciples, out of a desire to have others pay honor to you, serve you, or make material offerings to you

[86] Failing to dispel your laziness and the like

[87] Spending time with busy talk because you enjoy it

[88] Failing to seek the meaning of meditative concentration, out of a desire to hurt someone, or laziness

[89] Failing to purge yourself of the meditation obstacle of the pair of restless desire and missing something or someone

[90] Failing to purge yourself of the meditation obstacle of feelings of malice about someone

[91] Failing to purge yourself of the meditation obstacle of the pair of drowsiness and mental dullness

[92] Failing to purge yourself of the meditation obstacle of attraction to objects of the senses

[93] Failing to purge yourself of the meditation obstacle of unresolved doubts

[94] Considering the pleasant sensation of meditation to be an important personal attainment

[95] Rejecting the way of the listeners

[96] Making efforts in the scriptural collection of the listeners, when you have an opportunity to exert yourself in the scriptural collection of the bodhisattvas

[97] Making efforts in non Buddhist texts where no efforts should be made

[98] Being attracted to non–Buddhist texts, even in a case where one must make efforts

[99] Rejecting the greater way by discounting any part of the scriptural collection of the bodhisattvas by saying, "This part is not as good"

[100] Rejecting the greater way by discounting any part of the scriptural collection of the bodhisattvas by saying, "The composition at this point is inferior"

[101] Rejecting the greater way by discounting any part of the scriptural collection of the bodhisattvas by saying, "The author of this part was not the best"

[102] Rejecting the greater way by discounting any part of the scriptural collection of the bodhisattvas by saying, "This part won't contribute to the welfare of living beings"

[103] Praising oneself out of pride or anger

[104] Criticizing others out of pride or anger

[105] Not going to hear the Dharma out of pride or laziness

[106] Focusing on the vessel and the letters, by focusing on the teacher and not the teaching

[107] Failing to assist someone in need who is just undertaking a particular task, out of anger or laziness

[108] Failing to assist someone in need who is trying to get somewhere, out of anger or laziness

[109] Failing to assist someone in need who is trying to learn a language, out of anger or laziness

The Book

[110] Failing to assist someone in need who is trying to learn a skill (as long as it is not something harmful), out of anger or laziness

[111] Failing to assist someone in need who is trying to protect their belongings, out of anger or laziness

[112] Failing to assist someone in need who is trying to fix a split between people, out of anger or laziness

[113] Failing to assist someone in need who is planning a virtuous event of some kind, out of anger or laziness

[114] Failing to assist someone in need who is undertaking some more general virtue, out of anger or laziness

[115] Failing to serve the sick, out of anger or laziness

[116] Failing to make some attempt to remove the suffering of those who are blind, deaf, handicapped, weary from travelling, tormented by any of the five mental obstacles, haunted by thoughts such as malice toward someone, or suffering from defeat at the hands of someone else

[117] Failing to give good reasons to those who are acting in a dangerous way, out of anger or laziness

[118] Failing to repay someone who has helped you, by helping them back, out of a desire to hurt someone or out of laziness

[119] Failing to dispel another person's grief, out of a desire to hurt someone or out of laziness

[120] Failing to give money or other material things to some-one who wants them, out of a desire to hurt someone or out of laziness

[121] Failing to fill the needs of your circle of disciples, out of a desire to hurt someone or out of laziness

[122] Failing to get along with someone, out of a desire to hurt someone or out of laziness

[123] Failing to praise someone's good qualities, out of a desire to hurt someone or out of laziness

[124] Failing to cut someone off when the time has come to do so, out of mental afflictions or laziness

[125] Failing to use your supernormal powers to threaten someone or such when needed

C. SECONDARY OFFENSES AGAINST THE PRECEPTS OF THE PRAYER FOR THE WISH FOR ENLIGHTENMENT

[126] Failing to support those whom it would be proper to support, with Dharma

[127] Failing to support those whom it would be proper to support, with material things

[128] Failing to let go of your anger about something some one else had done to hurt you

[129] Discriminating between people, in the sense of liking some and disliking others

[130] Failing to take yourself to a holy Lama

[131] Giving up the practice of learning

[132] Giving up the practice of contemplating upon what you have learned

[133] Failing to have helping others in mind as you partake of food or clothing or any other thing that you make use of

[134] Engaging in any virtuous activity without having in mind the wish to reach enlightenment for the sake of all living beings

D. THE BLACK AND WHITE DEEDS

[135] The black deed of intentionally deceiving your Lama, or those to whom we make offerings, or any such person, by lying to them

[136] The white deed of never intentionally speaking a lie, even if only in jest, to any single living being there is

[137] The black deed of causing another person to regret some virtuous thing they have done

[138] The white deed of bringing a person that you are cultivating to strive for total enlightenment, rather than bringing them to the path of the lower way

[139] The black deed of saying something unpleasant to a bodhisattva out of anger

[140] The white deed of trying to conceive of every sentient being as the Teacher himself, and to see all beings and things as totally pure

[141] The black deed of acting in a devious way with any living being, without any sense of personal responsibility for their enlightenment

[142] The white deed of maintaining an attitude of total honesty toward every being, free of any kind of deception

IV. THE FIVE VOWS OF A LIFETIME LAYPERSON

[143] Not killing a human or a human fetus

[144] Not stealing anything of value

[145] Not lying about your spiritual realizations

[146] Not committing adultery

[147] Not taking alcohol or intoxicants

Colophon

This booklet is from a class taught by Geshe Michael Roach in New York City, August 1999, with slight editorial changes by Gail Deutsch.

Thanks to Peter Green for helping transcribe this tape, Pat Turrigiano for editing, Judy Tarbell and Peter Johnstone for layout, Nile Sprague for technical assistance, and John Stilwell for all of his advice. This teaching was compiled by Gail Deutsch, and I apologize for any mistakes it may contain. May the virtue accumulated in reading this book and following this precious advice cause all of us to create our Buddha paradise.

For information on other teachings by
Geshe Michael Roach,
including recordings of his teachings,
please contact: www.theknowledgebase.com

For more information about Geshe Michael Roach,
including his teaching schedule,
please contact: http://geshemichaelroach.com
Asian Classics Institute Home Study: www.acidharma.org
Diamond Mountain: www.diamondmtn.org
Global Family Project: http://globalfamilyproject.org
Other projects: www.world-view.org